Privatized

BANKING

Privatized

BANKING

BECOMING THE
SOLE PROPRIETOR OF
YOUR OWN BANK

LUCIEN STEPHENSON, CKA®

XULON PRESS

Xulon Press
2301 Lucien Way #415
Maitland, FL 32751
407.339.4217
www.xulonpress.com

© 2020 by Lucien Stephenson, CKA®

All rights reserved solely by the author. The author guarantees all contents are original and do not infringe upon the legal rights of any other person or work. No part of this book may be reproduced in any form without the permission of the author. The views expressed in this book are not necessarily those of the publisher.

Unless otherwise indicated, Scripture quotations taken from the Holy Bible, New International Version (NIV). Copyright © 1973, 1978, 1984, 2011 by Biblica, Inc.™. Used by permission. All rights reserved.

Printed in the United States of America.

Library of Congress Control Number: 2020909233
ISBN-13: 978-1-54567-873-2

ACKNOWLEDGEMENTS

Many thanks once again to Tamma Ford. I could not have completed this book without her assistance.

DEDICATION

As all fathers know, everything changes once there is a child in your life. This book is dedicated to my son Kelechi Stephenson and my daughter Adora Stephenson.

My children were named well: Adora means *beloved daughter of all*, while Kelechi means *thank God*. May this scripture guide them always:

> *"Therefore, my brothers and sisters, make every effort to*
> *confirm your calling and election.*
> *For if you do these things, you will never stumble, and you*
> *will receive a rich welcome into the eternal kingdom of our*
> *LORD and Savior Jesus Christ."*
> 2 Peter 1:10-11

ABOUT THE AUTHOR

Lucien Stephenson is a member of ***Kingdom Advisors*** where he has earned the professional designation Certified Kingdom Advisor™ (***CKA***®).

He is an avid student of Biblical scripture and operates a faith-based business as owner/president of ***Stephenson & Company*** – a strategic planning and wealth management firm based in Dover Ohio – which advises individuals and organizations.

He is a graduate of Kent State University, with a Master's Certificate in Financial Planning from The Ohio State University and a Six Sigma Green Belt Certificate from Villanova University.

Lucien is an author of three other books available on Amazon:

1. *A Daily Bible Reading Calendar*
2. *The Little Book on Giving: Gain It All by Giving It All*
3. *Total Clarity: Understanding the Four Keys to Successful Investing*

TABLE OF CONTENTS

PART 1 1

Chapter 1: How You Are Missing Out on Great Wealth 5
Chapter 2: Who Is This Tool For? 11
Chapter 3: Who Should Not Plan on Using This Information or This Tool? . .13
Chapter 4: What Are the Advantages to Me of Doing This? 15

PART 2 19

Chapter 5: What Is This Miracle Money-Management
and Wealth-Building Tool? 21
Chapter 6: How It Works – The Mechanics of This Instrument 25
Chapter 7: The Many Ways You Can Use It 39
Chapter 8: More Advantages to Using These Policies 49
Chapter 9: Charts & Scenarios 59
Chapter 10: Case Studies – Real People, Real Money, Real Life Stories 71

Conclusion 83

PART 1

"A feast is made for laughter, wine makes life merry,

and money is the answer for everything."

Ecclesiastes 10:19

The financial industry has not been good to Main Street investors and savers in the last 20 years, with very few exceptions (which I have been happy to create for the clients of my own practice).

I realize that there are as many versions of this story as there are people who earn, invest and save money in this country. However, if you are reading this book you are probably over age 18, and have significant indirect and direct experience with the economic and financial events of this millennium. You might have parents or friends who lost their retirement funds – their entire wealth – in this millennium's two crashes.

The Dot-Com crash opened the Millennium with millions of Americans going from a 'plush' stock market account to 'crushed' account.

Only a few short years later, with a majority of ordinary investors still playing catch-up on their Dot-Com losses, the mortgage and financial industry blew up in a different way, with millions of Americans' life savings and wealth evaporated, their jobs withdrawn, and their homes lost in all that madness and mayhem. It was a devastating time for millions of families.

Many would say things just haven't "gotten back to normal" at all since these 2 events - especially since we are in a third wealth-crushing event called the COVID-19 pandemic. Certainly some have preserved their pre-COVID wealth. Are these people an exception to a widespread rule?

After the earlier Dot-Com dive, but especially in the aftermath of the Great Recession, many young people just leaving college with their degree in hand had few opportunities to secure seriously paid job positions in fields they'd trained for. In spite of their desire and need to get to work and to pay back their student loans, there were no job offers. They ended up back at their parents' house, often with a crushing student loan repayment schedule and far too little cash to pay it off.

Again, exceptions prove out this generalization. My point is that for any given generation – any of us at some point in our adult lives – there will be crises, busts, crashes and recessions and devastating losses to handle. There will also be the corresponding smooth sailing, boom times, and inflationary periods as well – which present different investing and saving challenges to be sure!

No Predicting!

So here we are in 2020, and we don't know what's around the next corner for us, financially or economically speaking. What I can tell you is that no one can predict the future. I can tell you, though, that the stock markets will remain as volatile as they ever have been historically, for better and for worse (depending on your preparation for such shifts), and we have more recessions and inflationary periods in store during our lives.

The Big Banks, Wall Street and financial and all our lending institutions will still be as self-centered and corporate-profit-making-focused as ever, to our disadvantage as mainstream retail customers. In fact, since this century's Great Recession hit us, banks simply don't want middle-class Americans as clients anymore. We're not worth their time or trouble. The proof? It is in how low an interest rate they offer us for blocking our money in one of their savings or CD accounts, and how high an interest rate they charge us when we wish to borrow money from them (if they even 'approve' us for that loan … and they do so less and less often).

With the tool I am going to be presenting, we can now tell those institutions, "Two can play that game! Turnabout is fair play!" The Big Banks and lending institutions are not worth your trouble anymore, either! And that is a clue to what this entire book will be about, so stay with me.

True Diversification

As we have learned, even the most educated investor always needs to be a little nervous about the state of his or her nest egg – whether retirement is decades away or just a couple of years down the road. Diversification is fine, and I believe in it! However, most diversification that is offered to Main Street savers and investors like you is at the mercy of the next crash, the next recession, the next upheaval to our economy.

You should be big on diversifying your assets – but make sure that it is true diversification! Your job (or your single business) should never be your only means of income. You are almost obligated to own real estate, either in the form of your primary residence or some investment/rental income property (even in partnership with co-owners). You should have money in the stock market, whether bonds or blue-chip stocks. Within that diversified portfolio, you should have at least three months of living expenses for emergencies – ready cash, secure and safe and available.

As a great way to diversify, I need to state and restate that this magical money-managing, wealth-building tool I'm about to reveal is _not tied to the stock market_. It is separate from those markets and distinct in how it earns. And that is one of the best reasons most of my clients can think of to use this instrument – it is automatic diversification (aka protection of assets from risk) from the stock exchanges.

If you have not yet put in place a way to protect yourself in all cases from a market dive, against a recession period, against any sort of costly personal disasters such as a high cost medical crisis – you are really missing out. And if you have a business that may not be particularly recession-proof (and how many of them really are?), you also might wring your hands about how to protect it and ensure its longevity through thick and thin.

Let's look now at what it is exactly that you have been missing out on.

CHAPTER 1

HOW YOU ARE MISSING OUT ON GREAT WEALTH

"Ship your grain across the sea;

after many days you may receive a return."

Ecclesiastes 11:1

Even if you have a number of diversified investments, you are missing out on great wealth! There is a hole in your knowledge about money – especially as regards wealth-building, borrowing and lending.

Let's look at the investment vehicles that most people use. **50%** of adult Americans have money in the stock markets. About **25 million** Americans still benefit from a corporate or military pension plan. But only **500,000** Americans are using this much, much better tool. That means that only one-fifth of 1% of our total population and only two-thirds of 1% of Americans over age 18 is using this incredible tool – what an Elite Club!

And the surprise is this: This much better tool is legally, easily available to every adult! You can join this *Less-Than-1%-Club*.

What Messed Things Up for Us?

What messed things up, as a first example, was government. Now, I am neither for or against any particular action of the government, and that is not my point. In the post-WWII years, western governments – Europe, the US and Canada – sped up the development of ways that individual workers could save money for later, elder years. Corporate America expanded their offer of 401k (and other types of tax deferred) accounts; unionized industry ramped up their pension schemes; the US military had been using the pension approach for centuries and carried on with it.

Pension monies and your 401k monies are mostly invested in stocks. The Stock Market Professional just loves this! In spite of their oft-repeated hype to the contrary and taking all the boom and bust cycles into account, the S&P has performed at ONLY about 2% per year over its history. So even if you were smart with your 401k allocations, you were not doing well. And when you read about this other tool's results, you will be devastated when you put them in contrast with your own investments' profit record. Sorry, but it's the true, and I am about to help you fix all that.

Forgotten fact: Our grandparents knew about this high-performing tool and commonly used it – in the middle decades of the 20th century – in <u>all</u> the ways I will be presenting in the coming chapters.

What happened then, that we don't even know the name of it today, in this age of 'financial savvy and sophistication'?

The Internet happened. Wall Street and our stock market brokers went digital. They made it easy for each adult American to open a stock market account and (totally with online resources) invest in stocks, treasury notes, bonds and stock options. Suddenly, we were able to do this all on our own. See Scottrade, E*Trade,

TDAmeritrade and others like them. They've attracted millions of us and allow us to invest our bucks for ourselves at little cost.

But we also have little return or profits! We have not become very good at this investing online thing! We are so bad at this goal of profiting from our stock picks that 95% of us with such an account consistently lose money (lose our principle) or make only 2% or less if we are 'in the black'. And getting a full-service stock-broker does not (I repeat: does NOT) improve our profits. Nor does holding any mutual funds. In fact, we might as well open another savings account or get another Certificate of Deposit (CD) at our corner branch bank. And those pay less than 1% per annum as I write this in 2020.

Market volatility gives us nightmares because we don't understand how to use it in our favor. When the stock market crashes – and let's face it, it periodically does, and will again – we panic. We get out of the market by *selling* our shares. With the fear emotions that kick in at the time of a crash, we never seem to remember the rule to '*buy low* and sell high'. When the market takes a dive, we should be *buying* at 'thrift store prices (and then happily wait for the market to go up again, as it will). Instead, we are *selling* low and we lose our shirts! We do not understand how to make this up-and-down volatility work for us; we do not understand that fear and greed make us buy and sell at precisely the wrong times! And yet, we always seem to be willing to start over again, making the same old mistakes with the same old kinds of stocks. Whether we are just terrible at stock picking or insist on buying high and selling low … our hard-earned cash is out the window.

It gets worse.

If you own a business, you already cringe at what I'm going to say: If your credit is awful, or the economy is in recession (not so very long ago), or your business cash flow is not keeping up (as in so many cases in 2020 with the COVID-19 business shutdowns) - you are stuck. You cannot easily (or at all) access bank credit (aka cash money), so might not be able to meet payroll, upgrade that regulated piece of medical equipment on time to meet your licensing obligations, or pay your vendors… Crunch time.

Those **500,000** people I named? That *Less-than-1%-Club*? Recessions fly by them – they don't even notice it. Not in their personal lives, not in their businesses. They don't feel the financial pinch, much less any major crash. They don't fear for their jobs. They don't glue themselves to their stock report monitors. They don't sweat it in their businesses (even those that are not particularly 'recession-proof').

In these pages, you will learn what they have learned and be able to step into a brand-new 'relationship' with money.

Diversification

Whether you have been earning loads of money or a modest (or even irregular) salary, I'm guessing you have been saving some of it or even investing it. Otherwise, you wouldn't be reading this book.

I'd like to point out (gently) that no matter how diversified your investments, they are not providing the best return or tax picture that is readily available to you through this other terrific tool!

No matter how much cash you believe you are socking away for your own retirement or for your kids' college, or for that replacement car or just a rainy day, that cash of yours is just not <u>earning</u> as much as it could be and thus is not serving you as completely and abundantly as it could.

Do what a **half-million people** in-the-know are doing – put your cash in the *<u>right money-managing, wealth-building tool</u>*.

How Do You Use Money?

Think, as you turn these pages and learn about this tool and its terrific potential, of all the ways you use money.

If you are in business at this time, the list is probably long! But it also is when you are a parent or grandparent. When you are a single individual needing to fend for your own needs all the way through your elder years. When you love your 'stuff' and buy big-ticket items for yourself or spouse or kids. When you yearn for a bigger-ticket item like a vehicle, a home, a boat, a big world cruise...

I will leave you with this thought:

> # YOU FINANCE EVERYTHING THAT YOU BUY.

You are paying interest to someone (on a bank or auto loan; on a credit card). And, when sitting on the wrong side of the lending and borrowing table, you are losing an interest rate advantage. (The advantage is this: your dividends are higher than the loan interest rate, so you win like the bankers do!). My goal is to get you that seat on the right side of the table!

Remembering that we finance everything is core to your success using this new tool, so I will circle back to this concept again and again. We will get more into the detail of that in a while, but first ... should you be the one even reading this book?

CHAPTER 2

WHO IS THIS TOOL FOR?

"Invest in seven ventures, yes, in eight; you do not know

what disaster may come upon the land."

Ecclesiastes 11: 2

Remember this: This new and highly effective tool is a Must-Use for everyone that <u>interacts with money</u> in ANY way.

Well. That could be the end of this chapter!

I mean simply that this book is for *you*. For everyone from mid-teens and older. Whatever your background or earnings level. For all of you, wherever you are in your 'story' with money right now.

This information is for people of any age who need to take financial care of themselves and loved ones – even if you haven't done so well so far on this score. Note that you can start using this tool <u>at any age, and even if you are already retired</u> – to great benefit.

This is for those who are ready to take control over your personal or family money matters, including your tax picture. You need this is you want to leave a legacy – whether to family members or other loved ones, to a charitable organization or a church.

It's for parents or singles who just want to know that your money is really working for you, not only throughout your active working lives but later, when you retire from the world of active work. It's for you who have experienced one (or more) wealth-destroying crash; moving forward you want to know the money you are saving now will be there when you want and need it.

It's for those of you operating – or yearning to launch or expand – any type of business. ANY type – a product-selling, service-providing, wholesaling, retailing, digital, brick-and-mortar activity in any industry you can name.

As a business owner, you can likewise use this tool to fully, truly control your own business financing needs. I am a faith-focused financial professional and I use it to create a legacy I can leave my church, and for all sorts of family and business needs. I will be sharing Case Studies in a later chapter to illustrate how professionals use – or should be using – this tool. I'll also be sharing various ways of applying the power of this tool in your own personal and family life.

Finally, this information is for those who are ready for peace of mind regarding their financial stability and freedom, about their legacy, their retirement years, their business's ability to thrive in all economic climates…

Do you see that you cannot stop reading yet?

CHAPTER 3

WHO SHOULD NOT PLAN ON USING THIS INFORMATION OR THIS TOOL?

"If clouds are full of water, they pour rain on the earth.

Whether a tree falls to the south or to the north,

in the place where it falls, there it will lie."

Ecclesiastes 11:3

There will always be people who are happy to acquire information yet reluctant to act on it for their own benefit. That's fine.

There will always be people who hear (and believe!) that "you'll lose your shirt" in the stock markets because it is "so volatile" – yet these same people have all their retirement money and most of the rest of their saved cash in the markets, managed by a broker they hardly know. That's fine, I guess, too.

Let me say this: If you are happy to let your accountant and banker and stock-broker "take care of the money stuff" for you, and to just follow their direction, you don't want this information of mine at all.

Anyone who doesn't care about the profitable returns on the financial or other investments you have made in your lifetime need not continue reading. If returns on your savings or CD accounts at the bank make you yawn with disinterest ... if the returns on your individual stock accounts are no big deal to you ... if the returns on your pension and 401k or related types of IRS-approved accounts are mystifying to you and you just give up on understanding or improving them ... well, I don't have anything for you here! You are already doing what you want to do. Give this book away.

This book isn't for people who don't care how much tax you will pay year-after-year or over your lifetime, or that the amounts seem to increase year after year. It isn't for anyone who is more comfortable looking at the deep loss on your stock investment statements, even in booming economic times, than learning how to improve it.

And nothing I can say in these pages will be for anyone still at ease with the ill-performing traditional mainstream investment instruments and with the over-large tax burden that results.

If you just want to continue 'stressing out' about money in your everyday life ... if you are happy to keep panicking about how to fund your retirement (if you even can) ... if you do not mind fretting about paying the tax man on time ... I also don't have much of interest for you.

If the above statements don't describe you, stay with me for a few more pages, because you are in for a whole basketful of benefits, and they are right around the corner.

CHAPTER 4

WHAT ARE THE ADVANTAGES TO ME OF DOING THIS?

"Whoever watches the wind will not plant;

whoever looks at the clouds will not reap."

Ecclesiastes 11:4

You'll need to hold your breath for just one more chapter to find out exactly what this Miracle Tool is, because I need you to realize how many advantages, benefits, efficiencies and applications this miracle tool present to everyone who owns it – and ***uses it to its full potential as designed.***

You know we are talking about money – it's my job, I do it all day, and I know a secret that you are about to learn. If you are tired of not having mastery, really genuine mastery and control over your hard-earned money, you need this knowledge. Again, it's fine to acquire knowledge, but if you do not maximize its benefits through action, what is the point?

So, we need to know what the main benefits are – and all the secondary ones, too (though I am of the opinion that they should all be put in the #1 spot on the list)!

Advantages and Benefits

The advantages and characteristics of this miracle are – you will soon see for yourself – true <u>money-game changers</u> for you.

This is my top short list of benefits: *Guarantee of stated returns, safety of all principle, liquidity of all cash, exponential growth, and personal control.* Right there is more than we are offered by any mainstream bank or stock market investment!

But let's get into others:

1. Think about it: In our country's history, there have been over **90 economic 'slumps'** – when everyone, or nearly so, seems to lose their wealth and has to start over again. When businesses that are not particularly recession-proof, or which depend 100% on their customers' disposable income to create their own, typically fail. Know this: Those who use this tool never lose a nickel during any crash, and the support their businesses receives (by using this tool) keeps them going and glowing with health! **These people's savings were not only NOT wiped out, they GREW** – all because of the guaranteed and built-in attributes of this miracle tool. (And no, they did not short the market).

2. This is the biggest deal for many people: The earnings you make and the withdrawals you take are **100% tax-free** when structured properly. More on that outstanding (and to some, unbelievable) advantage later.

3. You can tell your banker, "Thanks, but no thanks." **You will never need your bank or its resources again** once you get going with this tool. Don't you feel like a beggar going to your bank to request a loan? Don't you feel like they control the amount of the loan (through the high interest rate which they

impose and which is a killer, as well as through how much you are approved for based on your current income/earnings/credit rating)?

4. Speaking of life savings, people in the *Less-Than-1%-Club* have totally stopped placing any part of their money in non-performing, shaky or 'too good to be true' investment instruments. This miracle tool delivers as much as **40 times the returns** those TV gurus spout off about, in a way that keeps every penny of principle and gains safe. Because of the structure built into this instrument, your saved money grows at a higher-than-market percentage rate – and because of the way your money is treated, it *also* **super-charges the power (end results) of compounding**.

5. This instrument of ours has **increased in value every year for over 160 years**. There is no economic shakeup it hasn't survived! We can safely say it is here for the long haul for each of us, too.

6. You enjoy **total flexibility** of access: same-business-day availability and no-questions-asked access to all your own money, with no approvals or inter-rogations involved.

7. It is **transparently clear what you own, what its value is** today, and what its value will be at any given time in the future. You might make an error of its future value – but on the low side!

8. **You control** what to do with your cash. The cash that is already yours is **available to you instantly**, as you need or want it.

9. **Take any loans out of your equity**, as if you were your own banker (because you are). Borrow from yourself for any need and with no explanations to anyone – regardless of your credit history or approval status. That cash is instantly in your hand for your chosen purpose no questions asked. Borrowing at an unbeatable interest rate is your privilege, as is easily avoiding high bank/

credit card interest rates which are the scourge of the American family and the American business.

10. **Borrow from yourself** – without slowing down or jeopardizing the continuing growth of your investment. More on this miraculous aspect of this instrument later!

11. **Lower or eliminate the federal tax liability** on your gains – forever.

There is some additional detail connected to the items in my list, and we'll get to that. It is very simple, and that detail usually enhances the benefits I've named and makes them even more astonishing.

If nothing else, the words '**tax-free basis**' should grab your attention! But on serious reflection, can you state that any of the items above are true about <u>all of your money</u> … or is your money immobilized in a certain type of investment, tied up, locked in somewhere so that you don't have instant access? Is it sitting somewhere on a deferred tax holding pattern?

These are just a few highlights of the benefits and game-changing advantages of this tool, so let's now dive into what it is … and then, I'll tell you even more advantages that you will enjoy.

PART 2

"I applied my mind to study and to explore by wisdom
all that is done under the heavens.
What a heavy burden God has laid on mankind!"
Ecclesiastes 1:13

As I have hinted, this money-managing, wealth-building tool is 'sort of' a secret in that only about half a million Americans – much less than 1% of the adult population – have heard of it, much less are using it. Many more of us have some knowledge of IRAs, 401k plans, CDs at their bank, mutual funds, stock market accounts. But these latter tools are, sadly, mostly underperformers, in spite of the numbers of individuals subscribing to them!

This so-called miracle tool is indeed a specific and quite different money-management and wealth-building tool than any even the most informed of my clients have heard of. In fact, though I have been in the world of financial planning for two decades, it was from the Treasurer at the church I attend with my family that I first heard about this instrument! I then had to scramble to do the research and find out if what he was talking about was real, legal and usable by anyone (as he intimated) – and as astonishing in its outcomes.

19

He was right. And now I set up such tools for countless clients – including a physician's multi-location business (see her story in the Case Studies chapter) and that of other professionals, people I know from church, long-time clients of my own practice, and for my own family.

Any adult earning money can get this instrument properly designed and start using it immediately to manage money. It's not just for the wealthy. ***It's for those who are ready to <u>become</u> wealthy.***

Let's see what it is and how it works.

CHAPTER 5

WHAT IS THIS MIRACLE MONEY-MANAGEMENT AND WEALTH-BUILDING TOOL?

"As you do not know the path of the wind,

or how the body is formed[a] in a mother's womb,

so you cannot understand the work of God, the Maker of all things."

Ecclesiastes 11:5

T his tool is decidedly NOT sexy because its very name – while a real mouthful – is ho-hum boring. Not catchy at all.

Nor is this tool innovative, at least not in the sense that it is a brand new, shiny creation. It has been around for *two centuries* or more, so it's definitely not new.

It is not mainstream, either. Even professionals with a career in this specific industry (myself included, until that chat with the treasurer of the church I attend with my family) don't know how to set it up, use it, recommend it or talk to you about it. It baffles them. And that is why there is a *Less-Than-1%-Club* of people owning this tool.

Lastly, it is most definitely not a get-rich-quick tool, although it is definitely a 'get-richer-than-your-dreams' tool if you use it in the prescribed way (which is straightforward and easy to learn).

This miracle I've been speaking of? It is the …

Participating Dividend-Paying
Whole Life Insurance Policy

Settle down with that mouthful of words, while I make a few points:

- This is indeed a **whole life insurance policy with little-known *riders* added to it**. It only seems to resemble all *whole life* insurance policies (as opposed to *term policies*, which is not at all what we want here). It is quite a bit different in its results and usage.

- Like other whole life insurance policies you take out on yourself or a loved one, it **pays a Death Benefit** to the named beneficiaries. It is a true life insurance policy in that regard, and you will keep it current with that in mind. In all other regards, it differs from your 'vanilla, off-the-shelf' policy in ways you will see in this and the next chapter.

- I say '**participating**' because you participate in the insurance carrier's profits. There are two types of whole life policies – those issued by *stock*-based companies and those which are *mutual* in nature. 'Mutual' (as in 'mutual funds') means that you participate in the profits – the profits are shared with you in the form of **dividends**. By legal definition, dividends are 'an overpaid (insurance) premium' and not a windfall profit your investment has made. Thus, it is 'returned' to you … **tax-free**.

- Not all life insurance **companies** offer **this form of policy**, and – as odd as that seems – that has always been true. That means you'll need to know which few companies among the thousand or so major insurance carriers actually offer it.

  - o Likewise, not all insurance *agents* are in the know. Most agents placing life insurance don't even know about this form of policy, much less how to write it up properly, as I've said. I'll point you to those that know, who get it right and can explain it to you with clarity and full transparency so that you can 'operate' it as easily as your own automobile!

- It requires you to **think in the long-term**. As I have said, this is a safe and wise money-manager and a guaranteed wealth-builder when used as designed, but it is not an overnight thing (though in my case studies, you will see how it can nonetheless be beneficial to you quite quickly). This said, even if you are already retired, and even if you are in your 70s or 80s, you can also do this type of long-term thinking. I'll show you how.

At Last – Become Your Own Banker

The title of my book promised that you could become your own banker. Here is where you learn how to do that – and how *easy* it actually can be!

You will see, in fact, that you are <u>not</u> a *salaryman banker.*
You are the *sole proprietor of your very own bank.*
You are the *sole owner.*

You are the *sole borrower.*

You are the *sole investor.*

And… You are the *sole lender you will ever again need!*

It is the *design* of the policy allows you to become your own banker, fulfilling <u>all</u> the roles of a traditional banker: holding your saved money for safe-keeping, paying interest on accrued sums, allowing you to take out loans (and always 'pre-approved'!), and to make high-return investments when they appeal to you.

But there is so much more *control* you can exercise!

If you use it as your **Dividend-Paying Whole Life Insurance Policy with Riders** as designed, you in effect ***become the sole proprietor of your own bank.***

It is your own bank: You are the depositor, the withdrawer and borrower, the lender, the lead strategist. The insurance company 'simply' administers it for you – and you are its owner, CEO and Chief Operations Officer.

Yes, it is a true life insurance policy. Yes, it pays a death benefit to your named beneficiary. And, yes, I'm going to show you how it can become your own highly, highly profitable money-managing, wealth-building bank.

CHAPTER 6

HOW IT WORKS – THE MECHANICS OF THIS INSTRUMENT

"Sow your seed in the morning,

and at evening let your hands not be idle,

for you do not know which will succeed,

whether this or that, or whether both will do equally well."

Ecclesiastes 11:6

Your cash value dividend-paying whole life policy, with just a twist or two (the riders), becomes your own private money-managing, wealth-accumulating bank! It does have a few rules to follow for creating such wealth-building tools and for using them. There are additionally a few 'best practices' to guide you in using the policy, all of which we will see to now.

Use it right – use it the way it was designed – and it will be a magical money-manager and wealth-builder for you and your loved ones.

Terminology First

Learn a few key terms now, and this instrument comes to life for you:

This '**Cash Value Whole Life Insurance**' is your '**Base Policy**'. You'll pay annual (or quarterly) premiums into it. It pays out a death benefit to the named beneficiary upon the insured's death. You have a contract which spells out premium and dividend amounts and all the details you and the carrier are agreeing to.

The '**Premium**' is your saved cash that you deposit into the policy at premium time. You may apply some of that premium to your rider. That increases the wealth-building power of the policy!

The '**Cash Value**' is the total amount of cash accrued in the policy and available to you at any time during the life of the policy as a policy loan.

The '**Cash Value**' also serves as your '**Collateral**' against a '**Policy Loan**', as I explain below. The cash value represents the total amount of loans that you may contract from the policy; it is the total amount you may borrow at any time. One of the unique features of this tool is that the cash value *is not touched* by taking a policy loan. It is the insurance company lending you its own, 'different' money.

'**Dividends**' are your portion of profits that the insurance company guarantees to pay to you annually and are calculated on your accrued cash value at the time of payment. The percentage rate is set annually and is guaranteed for the 12-month period. Another uniqueness of this tool is that, as your cash value increases, the dividend paid on it grows too – and may with time equal or exceed your premium amount.

'**Interest**' is the nominal amount you pay back on a policy loan. You do pay the interest rate amounts to the insurance company - it is your 'cost of capital' - yet it is not going to be anywhere near the interest percentage your local bank will charge you. Far from it! What is more, it is typically less than your policy dividend rate.

'**Riders**' are attached to the base or main policy. These riders are like mini-insurance policies.

- One rider is a **PUAR** - Paid Up Additions Rider.
- The other rider is in fact a **Term Life Insurance** policy! The Term rider is primarily used to prevent the policy from becoming a MEC or Modified Endowment Contract (described in the next chapter) and for fulfilling the need for true life insurance.

The Policy

You contract for a "cash value dividend paying whole life insurance policy with riders". You will be adding "Paid Up Additions Riders" and a "Term Insurance Rider". That is the basis for the magic.

Note: You cannot start with a term life insurance policy and add these riders and achieve the same wealth-building outcomes. You cannot start with universal life or indexed universal life insurance and add these riders. *You must begin with a dividend paying whole life insurance policy from a mutual insurance company that can add these riders to the policy.*

You are accruing cash value with every premium you're paying in and with every additional dollar amount you may choose to pay in to your policy up to the maximum allowed. You direct a portion of your premium to the 'paid up additions rider' and to the 'term rider'. This is automated for you.

You build pretty significant cash value over, say, 2-5 years. From that time onward, you have the ability to take out a **Policy Loan**, which never affects your cash value amount. Why not? You are <u>not withdrawing</u> from your cash value pot at all. The insurance company lends you the amount from its own capital. Thus, the growth of that cash value continues, fully intact – uninterrupted. The uninterrupted payment of dividends to you in any year you are paying back such loans is guaranteed (you do not forfeit it just because you have taken a loan).

You have the ability to take a policy loan for a known low interest-rate to create passive income elsewhere, or to seize an opportunity for a higher return opportunity. You can do this while preserving your entire account value its growth and dividends, and preserving (even growing) your death benefit amount.

Because of your ability to take out a policy loan up to the amount of your cash value, a straight withdrawal from your cash value is never necessary. Even when you have fully retired from the world of work, and you are using your policy's accrued cash value as your retirement income, you will go through the process of taking out a policy loan. You simply, at this later time in your life, do not pay it back. This naturally has the effect of decreasing the Cash Value (and the related Death Benefit) of the policy, so you'll only do it late in life.

The death benefit will be payable to your designated beneficiary or beneficiaries, as with any whole life insurance policy. The actual death benefit is paid to the beneficiary or beneficiaries, is not increased by the remaining cash value in the policy.

MEC or Modified Endowment Contracts

Since these policies are created to be tax-free up to a certain dollar value only, (above which the IRS will call them an **MEC** or Modified Endowment Contract and they become taxable instruments), you may wish to create two or more policies to fulfill your needs. Just as a bank can open new branch offices, *you can own any number of policies* on yourself if you are in good health and qualify. If your health does not allow you to qualify for such policies you can still be the owner of the policy, by ensuring another individual's life (your spouse, your children or other close family member).

Why is this thing called an MEC even involved in a life insurance scenario? In the 1980s when interest rates were high, wealthy Americans would hide a lot of money in any number of whole life policies that paid 13% dividends. Remember that the principle and gains of your policy become cash value that is usable as loans from the life insurance company - tax-free. So back in the day, the government was not happy that the wealthy were side-stepping their 'tax obligation' in this way! That is when the MEC limits were set in stone.

If we have lots of cash value and a low death benefit on a single policy, there's a chance that you can become a MEC. The life insurance companies I work with will return to you any overpayment of premiums in order to avoid reaching the MEC limit OR until the threat of MEC is dissipated after seven years of policy ownership. Then the IRS would say that you have a modified endowment contract and not a life insurance policy, and tax the amounts put in the policy. Once your policy becomes a MEC designation, that can never be undone; the IRS is firm on this. When it becomes a MEC, your whole life policy is now treated as a taxable or tax-deferred retirement vehicle (like a 401k and similar) so even your policy loans will be taxed – just as when you draw money from your IRA or 401(k). All you need to do is contract for additional policies to avoid reaching that MEC limit – it's that easy to remain in a tax-free instrument.

The Insurance Companies

There are around one thousand major insurance companies today. The financially strongest life insurance groups in our country are, like all others, regularly audited by their home state insurance commissioner's offices – and by those of the different states in which they operate – which ensures that they maintain sufficient reserves to pay future claims and are on solid financial footing in all ways. The state insurance commissioner also issues a statement of policy owner protections for your information and comfort. In case of operating or solvency difficulties in any company, the state insurance commissioner will take over the operation of the company in the interests of the policyholders. Additionally, most insurance companies are audited by several independent rating companies. In the last 200 years of our economic history, through all types of economic weather, these insurance companies have been among the most stable businesses in the nation.

Life insurance companies have **$4.5 trillion dollars invested** in our national economy. This puts them at the top of the list of sources of capital in our nation. They are taxpaying entities, which have collectively paid nearly up to **$20 billion in federal state and local taxes per year.** They are required to have a foundation of proven and safe liquid assets – in the industry, this is called Tier 1 capital.

Warren Buffet's Berkshire Investments company believes in the solidity of the industry so firmly that it owns several stock-based insurance companies (though it does not hold mutual based ones such as our policyholders require, it does show the value of the best companies in the industry).

Life insurance cash values serve as a source of available capital to all of us – private individuals, families, large and small businesses – and in a recent year, *$1.3 billion in life insurance policy loans* were outstanding. This should also be solid proof to you that this type of instrument is widely used by those policy owners in the ways I am discussing.

More on How It Works: A Big Picture

To build this money-managing, wealth-building vehicle, you start with the **no-frills** dividend paying whole life insurance policy I have described. It is a permanent, or cash value, policy. This is the base policy you start with.

The cash value can grow each and every year but is not guaranteed to do so. This said, all of the life insurance companies that I work with have never missed a dividend payment in over 100 years. by a predetermined amount which is specified in your contract. The cash value is guaranteed to equal the policy's death benefit in some specific future year. That future year is called the policy's maturity date.

You will need to take out a policy by an insurance company owned by policy-holders. This is called a *mutual*, or *participating* company, making you the policy-holder a participant in the company's profits. Those profits are paid to you annually and called 'dividends'.

Whole life insurance is considered from a mutual carrier is a 'participating' policy with advantages that are easy to understand. The biggest benefit is that in a mutual life insurance company (a common 'ownership' structure for life insurance companies) the whole life policy owners are actually the owners of the company. As an owner of the company, you have a right to participate in the profitability of the company. If you own a business as full owner or as a partner who only owns a percentage of the company, you are in the same situation. If you own, say, 10000 shares in a listed company on the stock exchange that pays a dividend, you are also in a position of partial ownership of that listed company and share in its profits year after year in the form of dividends. Having an insurance policy from a mutual insurance company, you have partial ownership of the company, and thus when the company makes a profit, you likewise get a share of it.

The reason you need to go to a specialist mutual insurance company – and a trained insurance agent – is because of the Paid Up Additions Riders, PUAR. These are the **frills** that will customize your plan and supercharge its ability to grow exponentially for you. You maximize the growth of your cash value without increasing your premium.

A term rider with the PUAR round out the *additions to the base policy* and are like miniature policies-within-the-base-policy that require only a one-time premium. The 'base' policy premium is the only premium you're required to pay.

More on Those Little-Known Riders

A few extra details about riders:

- First, the term rider will increase the premium payment or the cost of insurance per $1,000.
- Second, not everyone will have a term rider. It just depends on the cost and your need for actual life insurance. I will not add the term rider if the client has no need for additional life insurance and does not expect an increase in personal income in the future. The term rider raises your death benefit beyond what was established in the base policy (and that is your explanation for how – in our chapter of Charts – you see the death benefit increase so much)!
- Third, 50% of the premium goes into the base policy and 50% of premium payments will be added or go into the Paid-Up Additions Rider or PUAR.
- Finally, remember that you add term insurance *as a rider* to your base policy; this is quite different from taking out a separate term life insurance policy. *They serve to augment, turbo-charge and power your wealth-building, as*

the cash value grows and grows. The higher the death benefit, the more you can save into the cash value, and the growth compounds on larger and larger sums of money. With the PUAR and the term rider (as opposed to just a base policy), ***your money grows up to eight times faster in the first year!*** Super-charging is the way to go.

Written and used correctly, your policy earns and pays out to you in *tax free dollars*. Those 'riders' are indeed 'the twist or two' that make this an outstanding, even magical, vehicle not only for building sure wealth but for managing your cash needs throughout your life via policy loans. The riders are the key elements of a dividend-paying whole life insurance policy that allows it to work in the ways I have outlined (and more details to come on those).

The Paid-Up Additions Rider, or PUAR, and the Term Rider are vital to a policy that *turns you into the sole proprietor of your own bank.* It is in the riders that the magic happens. The riders are there to *maximize the growth of your cash value without increasing your premium.*

Think Long Term

You must agree to think and act for the longer term. Such an investment in yourself is not about running after high returns, but about building wealth in a sure footed, long-term manner.

It is about finally having your money 100% safe in all kinds of economic weather, guaranteed to grow exponentially when you use the policy as designed, with all the cash value in your total control and liquid (available to you at any time).

Owning one or more of this type of policy allows you to live a lifestyle which you have been working hard for (but perhaps not enjoying) anyway. Growing your money in this way allows you great flexibility and lots of options. You know where your money is at all times!

If you wish to leave a legacy to your children or to a meaningful charitable organization, this miracle wealth building tool can allow you to do it.

With a dividend-paying whole life insurance policy contracted with a mutual insurance company and written up with you by a specifically trained insurance expert who will specially design it for this purpose, you …

- Save your money into the policy by paying a known premium amount into it.
- A portion of the premium is applied to the riders.
- The payment of a pre-agreed, fixed and guaranteed premium amount is your annual minimum to keep the policy in good standing, **but you may pay in any additional sums you wish** (being mindful of the Modified Endowment Contract, MEC, limits), thus building the **cash value** of your policy … while also increasing the death benefit amount over time.
- The premiums are the same amount year after year, if you choose to pay in annually over the full period.
- Earn **dividends** on the cash value residing in the policy – the dividends are are not guaranteed s (e.g..: 6%) and is declared annually. The mutual life insurance companies I work with have consistently declared a dividend in all types of economic fair and foul weather. Your policy will be built at a dividend rate depending on the insurance company practices and when you contract the policy (economics), so please note that the dividend and interest rates cited in this book may not correspond to what your policy ends up offering you.

Keep in mind the rate varies, but once declared for that specific policy year, it will not change in that year. Borrow up to the amount of the cash value you have developed in the policy – without touching the cash value itself. How? The insurer is your actual lender. The cash value in your policy at the time is the ceiling of your loan amount – since the insurance company lends you its own money and **uses your cash value as collateral.** Your accrued cash value remains 100% intact and continues, uninterrupted, to grow and earn dividends throughout the months or years you are paying yourself back.

- Yes, you will be paying interest to the life insurance company. The insurance company cannot deny you the loan, because loan provisions are built into the life insurance contract. are in control just as a banker would be. There is a tried-and-tested way of repaying your loan that can additionally supercharge the growth of your funds, and we'll see that in a later chapter.

If you re-read this section, you will detect **a number of ways you control your money and still keep it growing.**

1. You can pay more into the policy each year than your minimum premium amount, and that additional money is likewise guaranteed to earn and grow.
2. You can roll your dividends back into your cash value, which is an excellent idea in the early years of the policy. Many people with dividend-paying stocks do this, buying more shares with the dividend amount – it is the same principle.
3. Whenever you get a windfall of cash – a job bonus, an inheritance, a banner year of profits in your own business, sold a property or big-ticker item you

won't be replacing, etc. – you can deposit it to grow your policy's cash value and starting earning on that money in a safe, guaranteed manner.

4. You can add money to the account beyond the pre-agreed interest rate on a loan you make to yourself. Your insurance specialist will suggest that you pay back in a commercial interest rate (which is always higher than the one you "charge yourself"). I will provide illustrations on this later.

The advantages of a policy of this design (dividend-paying whole life insurance with PUAR and term riders) are so amazing that most people don't understand it at first, second or even more readings! Let me reword it here before we move on:

The cash value, the money in the policy – the premiums and extra cash you have deposited in it year after year – is _your money_. You may withdraw it all. It is your money. Just remember that **you are a banker now, with a repository of cash to borrow from and spend elsewhere, or to borrow from and invest when you find a higher-return opportunity.** So, you take out a low-interest loan from the insurance company administering your policy (_and who cannot say No!_) with your cash-value as collateral.

It is the insurance company's money that is lent to you:

No cash is deducted from your policy's cash value in this scenario! It can therefore keep earning and growing – non-stop and continuously! That is how the policy is designed.

When you choose to over-repay your loan by paying a higher interest rate than agreed, as is permitted, you only add more to the cash value *of your policy. The over-payment is added to your cash value, not 'earned' by the insurance company.*

Remember that the insurance company also has to invest its own capital to grow and prosper so your loan is an opportunity for them to do this – meaning you are using/borrowing/repaying their money instead of your own. The only function of your own cash-value amount is to serve as collateral … and keep on growing!

Your loan is charged interest as in the traditional banking world, but at a lower than market rate. In fact, it is always lower than the dividend percentage your policy is earning. You keep earning more than you are paying out.

Your cash-value (equivalent to the 'principle' of your money) continues to earn its dividend and grow in ways the insurance company is taking care of as it invests its own capital.

Now You Are the Banker, Too

Your wealth is growing during the life of the loan through your premium and extra payments into the policy.

What This is NOT

This is not the ordinary usage most people make of life insurance. Note that not every insurance agent sells this or even understands how to write it up. Not every insurance company offers this magical wealth-building, money-managing tool.

As I have said, you need to contract such a policy from only a handful of mutual insurance companies who know how to write these policies with the necessary riders. You should consult a specialist in such tools and have everything explained to you (as with all contracts) before signing on the bottom line.

There is a big difference between 'participating' and 'nonparticipating' policies. A participating life insurance policy is one that receives dividend payments from the life insurance company. A nonparticipating policy does not have the 'right' to share in the insurance carrier's profits and won't receive that wealth-building dividend payment.

Chapter 7

The Many Ways You Can Use It

"Light is sweet, and it pleases the eyes to see the sun."

Ecclesiastes 11:7

Fund It First

The first order of business is to contract for your policy and pay premiums into it for a period of two to five years without otherwise touching the policy or its cash value.

The exception would be this: Add more than the premium amount any time you can. Add any windfall monies you have to the policy after paying the taxes on them, up to the legally allowed amount (so that it does not become an MEC, as previously discussed).

This windfall cash might include:

- a yearly bonus your company pays you
- a lump-sum inheritance amount you are bequeathed

- a cash insurance settlement (when you don't actually need the cash, such as in a personal injury case where the cash settled on you goes to pay those built-up medical expenses)
- bumper profits from your own business in a banner earning year
- tax refund amounts
- and (why not) the net amount of your lottery winnings!

Time to Think Like the Owner of a Bank!

Once you have some cash value built up in the policy, there are a number of *practical ways* you, the policy owner, can use your own money to be your own banker. These apply to personal, educational, professional or business scenarios. Since many policy owners think that earning a 4% dividend is a very low return, you might have your eye on valid high-return investment scenarios (where the investments are made by you personally or by a business you own) and need cash to take advantage of the opportunity. Let's look at some scenarios now (go to the Charts chapter, and to the Case Studies chapter, too, to see how the numbers can potentially play out).

Personal Uses

Let me just list the many, many ways an unmarried individual or a person with a family might need a lump-sum of cash beyond the everyday costs of living. Let me also remind you that whatever you purchase with your policy loans, it does not – repeat, does not – serve as the collateral for your loan! Your purchased item is not collateral and that represents good security. It is your Cash Value that is the insurance carrier's collateral.

- Pay down high interest, big credit card balances all at once or pay down another type of outstanding personal loan (such as auto loans) – pay it in full and never be in such debt again!

- Funding your own or one or more child's higher education (college tuition and school-related expenses and living costs)

- Purchasing one or more personal or family vehicles, and replacing them, say, once every four years or so (because you wish all your vehicles to be in safe condition)

- Buying a primary residence, whether condo or single-family home; paying off a current mortgage in one lump sum – and doing any of this cash-in-full, early, and once and for all

- Making major home improvements such as changes to remain up to code or remodeling for modernization, adding space to your house, etc.

- Vacation or second-home purchase

- Buying passive income rental real estate, whether commercial, multi-family or single-family properties – for your or your family's own account

- Any big-ticket item you wish to own, such as a sail/power boat, ATV and other recreational vehicles like snowmobiles or campers/recreational vehicles, scuba gear, a small plane, etc.

- Enjoying an extended overseas vacation, or periodic educational journeys for the whole family

- Medical bills – in spite of having terrific health insurance coverage (and especially if you do not have it), a medical catastrophe can suck up all the coverage you have and leave you to pay the difference. That can be thousands and tens of thousands of dollars you need to find! The cash value of your whole life policy is here for you to help cover some or all of that medical debt.

As you already know, many of these expenditures are typically made

1. On a high-interest-rate credit card

2. Through a high-interest-rate bank loan

3. Through a high-interest-rate financing company (auto loans)

4. Through a federally guaranteed loan that can never be cancelled, even due to bankruptcy (student loans and SBA loans for business are the best known)

5. From traditional savings accounts, which you set up for the purpose and fully withdraw from to buy the item (e.g.: your 'Christmas' account, for gifts and that trip to spend the New Year with family across country)

6. From IRS-tax-advantaged savings accounts (various educational or retirement types of accounts)

You no longer have to use these types of financing sources!

You are the bank. You are your own banker. You own the bank now. Being the sole proprietor really has its perks!

Professional Uses

Businesses need access to capital – as known as *ready cash*. Cash is the life blood of our businesses and our economy!

If any of you were active in the economy during this millennium's Great Recession, you know that capital availability all but dried up. The capital itself didn't go away! That is a misconception. But those who held it were cautious about lending it at any price. Even businesses with the best track records found they could not borrow money, and all too often their lines of credit were canceled as well.

Such events need *never* interrupt your business operations (or your peace of mind) again!

As your own banker, you can now access capital for purposes such as some or all of the following:

- Purchasing commercial real estate to operate your business from (whereby you also gain income by renting out the remaining spaces in it, while never again worrying about rent hikes to your own premises!)

- Buying high-ticket business/professional equipment rather than leasing it or borrowing from the bank to buy it (if the ownership of it makes tax sense and financial sense to your type of operation)

- Funding your business's cash flow needs in a temporary sales slump period or in an economic downturn when bankers' credit has dried up, etc.

- Meeting payroll in a crunch

- Paying vendor invoices when cash flow is otherwise tight

- Expanding your current business to multiple new locations

- Expanding your product lines through self-financed Research and Development (R&D); self-funding the manufacture of that new inventory

I believe you have understood, but I will restate it now, that you can achieve any of these personal or professional goals by taking out policy loans.

<u>Remember</u>: You can borrow up to the amount of the cash value of your policy at the time of the loan.

Remember: You are a private banker to your business now, and how does a bank make money? By charging interest on money it lends! You are thus also charging yourself (an advantageous) interest rate for the amount you borrow.

Remember: A borrower remains 'in good standing' with his lender by paying back the loan as agreed. Repayment must be on time and in full to ensure your creditworthiness. So, as you are both basically borrower and lender, you pay yourself back as agreed. (Yes, it is the insurance company who is officially the lender, but why risk your cash value – which stands as collateral – by not paying the loan back to the company in a timely manner?)

Some people forget this advantage: You are not reducing your cash value when you take out a policy loan. Your cash value is only your collateral, and as long as you repay the loan as agreed (and you would anyway wherever you borrow from), your cash value remains intact – earning dividends and growing in an uninterrupted manner.

Remember: When you take out a *policy loan* it has a very, very different effect on your cash value balance from *withdrawing* outright from your policy and not paying the amount back. Indeed, you may want to access your cash when you are in your later years with a plush Cash Value in the policy; this is more accurately called an 'unrepaid' policy loan. It is, in that instance, more like a straight withdrawal from any of your cash accounts at the corner bank; it is not like a traditional bank loan, in that you cannot default on your own non-repayment!

1. In a policy loan scenario, the insurance company is the legal lender and your policy's cash value is untouched. The cash value amount is unchanged and continues to earn that annual dividend – for uninterrupted compounding and growth.

2. In a pure withdrawal scenario, you are asking to be paid or sent an amount of money from your policy's own accrued cash value. The cash value amount is decreased by the amount of your withdrawal. Naturally, whatever you have withdrawn is no longer eligible for the dividend calculation. Growth stops.

Bottom Line: Do not *withdraw* your cash value but take out a *policy loan* with the cash value as collateral instead. Do this even in your later years, when you are calling on the policy cash value to fund your later, retirement costs of living (in this case, you simply do not pay the policy loan back, but let the cash value decrease).

A Word about Interest Rates & Returns

I have only mentioned interest rates a few times so far. The number one argument I hear from people about setting up a dividend-paying cash value whole life insurance policy as I have been describing is this: "But Lucien! I can get much better interest rates elsewhere, on other types of investments." (NOTE to those protesters: Read the Case Study by Todd Colucy in that chapter. He'll set you straight about 'returns'.)

First of all, perhaps you can find a better return, since Todd did! But I believe in diversification, and one or more of these cash value policies should be part of your portfolio, for the many reasons, uses and advantages they represent – not the least of which is certain wealth-building capacity.

Secondly, this tool is not primarily about chasing a number called a high rate of interest. Remember that I have very specifically been calling it a 'money-management and wealth-building' instrument. If I were being stubborn with you, I would state that most people – professionals and individuals managing their own money in the markets – don't know how to understand or survive 1) market volatility or 2) economic downturns. For proof, just ask the people around you how many lost the bulk of their stock portfolio in the Dot Com crash and how many lost their shirts in the Great Recession of this millennium, not to mention the more current COVID-19 economic market drop. I rest my case.

It is the trend to 'buy high and sell low' instead of the opposite that kills our chances to profit in the stock markets. Fear and greed make us ignore the value of volatility (rises and falls of the markets) or use it to our advantage. Because we are so emotional about our money and so reactive to shifts in the markets, we lose – sometimes losing everything (both paper profits accrued *and* our principle).

We also are incapable (professionals' assertions to the contrary) to predict the future, and so can't 'get our money out' before a market crash, nor know how long it will take to rebuild the funds we lost. Likewise, and because we don't have a crystal ball, when a recession hits, we are often too late in bolstering our businesses to take the hit and survive the storm … and risk losing it outright. We forget that not all businesses are of the 'recession-proof' type…

Getting a guaranteed 4% dividend year after year on your 'pot of money' is admirable, when compared to this lack of predictability!

For me – and it should also be so for you – it is about a consistently, exponentially growing pot of money which is absolutely safe from stock market and other economic fluctuations. Safe from fluctuations in the profits or losses of your business. Safe from interruptions to its compounded growth.

Back to interest rates and returns. How much of your money are you wasting right now? Remember that we are financing everything we buy – either through paying interest to have the thing, or on lost interest we are not earning on that money spent:

- Paying 10-30% interest to a credit card company on outstanding balances is a waste of your hard-earned money. We all agree. It need not be a fact of your financial life.

- Going to a financial institution and paying 13-14% on an auto loan because your credit score is not great? That also needs to be part of your past.

- Paying 8% on a student loan (federally guaranteed or not), and even more on the parental loans that supplement it, is paying too much.

- And, lest we forget 'the Big One' – most people with 30-year mortgages are paying double the sale price of their property. That was interest, and it all went to the lender.

Shouldn't the lender in those scenarios have been you?

So, when you state that a 4% dividend on your money is low, stop! Factor in the interest that you are *not paying elsewhere*. A policy loan will never charge more than your dividend rate in a normal economic environment. This means that you wipe out your credit card debt and never incur those double-digit rates again. That is money that never left your pocket (or your policy's cash value amount). Paying 14% on a car loan is no longer part of what you consider affordable; you take out a policy loan and generally pay less than your dividend percentage in interest. Fund your children's education as needed – but at your own low rate.

A bank savings account earns less than 2% everywhere in the land. Put that saved cash into your cash value policy and get a 4% dividend and even more exponential growth! Don't use the corner bank's savings accounts or CDs anymore – save for Christmas, that new boat, that annual vacation to Europe in your cash value dividend paying whole life insurance policy with riders – from now on. Lend to yourself. Let your money keep earning.

I cannot repeat this enough, because you cannot get it just anywhere, and it adds to your gains so very much: Everything in your dividend paying cash value whole life insurance policy (Permanent Life Insurance) is *growing tax free*.

The interest you saved in all those cases is sitting in your fat cash value policy, exponentially growing – and just waiting for you to use it for lifestyle purchases, true higher return investments you discover, for your business needs or new business opportunities.

Then, contrast this policy with your brokerage account, whether it is for your individual accounts or your 401(k). Yes, you may be quite good at growing your individual, self-directed accounts during any multi-year bull (rising) market. But none of us controls economic events like the sudden market drop we see with the COVID-19 pandemic news. But you don't really control your 401k account composition or timing; they are not usually self-directed accounts! Someone else administers it. Any stock market account can lose all its profits and gains from that bull market but also the principle you poured into it. We don't have crystal balls.

In a cash value policy, you never lose your principle; in fact, it only increases.

CHAPTER 8

MORE ADVANTAGES TO USING THESE POLICIES

"However many years anyone may live, let them enjoy them all.

But let them remember the days of darkness, for there will be many.

Everything to come is meaningless."

Ecclesiastes 11:8

D ividend-paying cash value whole life insurance – with those riders – is built for your success. It is designed with built-in benefits and guarantees:

- Your policy premium is guaranteed never to increase, and offers the predictability of a fixed cash amount to pay in each year/quarter

- The cash value you accrue grows by a guaranteed minimum, predictable amount each year

- It is also real-life insurance, meaning that the death benefit is guaranteed, and grows along with your cash value

- Presumably you can borrow against the accrued cash value at a lower interest rate than your dividend percentage, thus taking advantage of this 'spread', just like bankers do

- One or more policies are vehicles allowing you to be sole proprietor of your own 'lending institution' – cutting out the middlemen called bankers, credit card companies and finance companies, and to pocket the gains not paid out as high interest elsewhere

- Creates and provides a safe, reliable *and measurable* income for your retirement years with no fear of downward volatility or macro-economic disaster affecting the predicted amount – try measuring how much 401k retirement funds you'll have at retirement and you'll see by its very nature that you just can't do it!

Other Advantages

If you have read my book called ***Total Clarity***, you will recognize the following 4 reasons to start working with this wealth-building tool.

Investment Philosophy: This is the first pillar of my Total Clarity approach to investing. It is not only about how you will invest, but why you are investing at all. What are your financial goals, and what are your other goals' requirements for cash or funding? Going into a cash value policy tool as you have chosen to do means that you have answered these questions. You have determined that some of your needs and goals are long-term (funding your 2-year-old's college education; thinking at age 32 about having enough for your retirement at age 60 or 65, etc.). You are taking a long-term approach. In other words, you have a long-term investment strategy. The dividend-paying cash value whole life insurance tools suits you perfectly.

Clarity: You know exactly what you own and why you own it, and who you are partnered with in the ownership. You are working with a specially trained agent. You have chosen an outstanding insurance company experienced with and performing excellently with this tool. Your policy contract outlines your dividend rate quite clearly and states unequivocally that it remains unchanged during the life of the policy. You have added the riders that will serve to supercharge the exponential growth of cash you deposit in your account. Everything is clear from the start.

Flexibility: This is your money, and you have access to it all the time. There is no government-limited minimum or maximum contribution to your cash value life Insurance policy. The only constraint you may experience is how much death benefit the insurer grants, and whether you yourself are insurable or need to insure someone else. You have the flexibility to contribute as much or as little as you want (MEC is a tax-related constraint but it is the only one, which is easy to avoid by creating new policies as needed). You may borrow from your policy at will up to its cash value and your loans can be used for any personal or professional purposes you wish. You can own any number of policies that suit your Investment Philosophy (I know of people with 15 of them) and borrow from any/all of them up to your repayment capacity. You have the flexibility of paying back the exact amount of interest and loan principal agreed, or to increase that to supercharge your returns and growth.

Transparency: You know your exact dividend going into the policy and it does not change during the life of the policy. As policy owner, you designate a beneficiary and may change it anytime you require it. The insurance company issuing the policy is regulated, audited and monitored and has a very clear past history of success for you to track.

Your Greatest Advantage: Exponential Growth

We hear about the power of *compounding* all the time. This power is your ally in your cash-value policy's growth.

I've spoken about annual/quarterly premiums, accompanied by the annual dividend. The first you pay into the policy, and those *dollar amounts* are pre-determined and do not change during the life of the policy. The second you receive, and the percentage amounts are based on current cash value with the percentage amount being declared at the beginning of each year.

From the first premium deposited into your policy, you start earning and that cash will earn and grow into a larger sum, and the new sum will earn and grow through the dividends earned – in a snowball effect of increase.

To amplify this power of compounding is easy in such a policy, since when you take a policy loan all the interest increases your cash value. But there is another way to speed up the compounding: frontload the policy. The <u>sooner</u> you put bigger amounts of cash in a long-term investment instrument, the more compounding works to build your wealth.

Here are a simple couple of examples to remind you how compounding works:

- If you start with $2,500, earning a dividend of 6%, your first dividend payment will be on the $2,500. 6% of $2,500 is $150. Your new cash value is $2,650. The next year's 6% dividend will be calculated on $2,650 (not on the original $2,500). You end up with a $159 dividend amount (6% of $2,650), bringing you to a new cash value of $2,809. And so on through the years.

- If you start with $20,000, with a dividend of 6%, your first dividend payment will be on the $20,000 cash value. 6% of $20,000 is $1,200. Your new cash value is $21,200. The next dividend is paid based on the new sum of $21,200, and so on – the compounding happens in the same way through the years.

We keep in mind that this is an insurance policy, so you need to look at the charts coming up to see that the insurance pays itself off the top in the first year or two, so you really seem to start in the red. Rest assured, you catch up quickly! This is why it is typically advisable not to touch the policy's cash value in the first 2-5 years through policy loans. You are starting the compounding process in those years.

So, what happens if you put the total premium amounts into the policy in, say, the first three years? Your long-term policy has <u>more years</u> to use compounding and thus to earn you even more at the policy's maturity in both cash value and death benefit amounts. You will see three samples of how to fund your policy in the next chapter's charts:

1. Regular annual payment of the agreed premium amount until completion
2. Partially frontloading the policy with higher amounts of cash (greater than the premium) the first 2 years and continuing by paying the exact contracted premium amount the remaining years
3. Fully frontloading the policy to completion in the first 1-3 years and pay no more premiums at all during the remainder of the policy's life.

Depending on how you view compounding, and depending on how much cash you have or can divert (switch) from other placements, you will choose one of the above options to fund your policy.

Be creative! You may have lump-sums of cash you are not thinking about that allow you to frontload your policy and start compounding earlier and on larger sums. You can frontload your policy either fully fund or partially over a couple of years, if you:

- have significant rainy-day cash stashed in non-performing savings or CD accounts
- churn out a large salary and can redirect all/some of it to the policy
- earn a large commission and can redirect all or some of it to the policy
- plan on getting a big year-end bonus or profit-sharing sum
- wish to get away from uncertainty involved in stock-based accounts like mutual funds or 401k accounts (you cash out, pay the taxes due for early withdrawal or closure and put the net amount toward your cash-value policy premium)

How else is your cash value amount growing? When you take out a loan policy you are paying interest on it. The interest you pay back accrues to your cash value. And one more way to snowball your policy value? Don't just pay in the premium amount but up that you predetermined on contracting the policy but pay in up to maximum premium allowed (see Michael Anthony's use of this growth technique in the Case Studies chapter). This is stated in your policy so be sure to ask the agent how much it is.

Let's Talk Security

I've already addressed in a number of ways how your money is secure with such policies.

When you look around you, you realize that times are going to be rough for many people, financially speaking, at some point in their lives. You, too, perhaps. In this type of insurance instrument, your money is secure. It grows exponentially, tax-free, probate-free. The cash value will never go down *due to market volatilities*, as the stock market periodically will. It is distinct and unrelated to the stock exchanges and those fluctuations!

If you take out a policy loan from yourself, say to buy a car or put money down on a piece of real estate? Your real estate (your home, condo, or investment property) or vehicle is <u>not placed as collateral</u> on the policy loans. Since the purchased item is not the collateral on any policy loan, you don't have to worry about repossession or foreclosure on the item. That is an additional security!

It is your policy's Cash Value that serves as the loan's collateral. I want to make the point that whatever it is your policy loan is financing, it is secure. If you take out a loan in the amount of the vehicle purchase, finalize that purchase and take possession of the vehicle – you own it outright. You now have that policy loan to take care of. If you plan on paying the policy loan back as agreed and do so, all is well. Or, if your strategy is, for whatever reason, to not pay your own policy loan back or not pay it back in full (and that would be a shame), you forfeit that amount from your policy's Cash Value. You retain full ownership of that vehicle which you have paid in full. Your cash has financed that vehicle; if you do not pay yourself back for some strategic reason, your purchased vehicle remains secure. Likewise, for any other purchase made with the proceeds of a policy loan. No Repo' Man will be showing up at your door!

Now Let's Talk Taxes

I've already said some of this, but it always bears repeating. Another very, very real way that your policy's real value to you grows is through the *retention by you of all monies you would – with other investment vehicles – have usually paid to the government in taxes*. Growth inside the policy through the dividend is **tax-free**. This policy solution, when used as designed, is **a tax-free vehicle**!

If you are approaching an 'over-funded' ceiling on a policy (which amount has been determined by the IRS), but wish to keep on saving and growing your wealth, you simply contract for a second (third, fourth, etc.) policy. Thus, you avoid having the policy transmute into an MEC (Modified Endowment Contract) which is taxable. I know individuals owning 5-6 policies and some with up to 15!

Borrowing against your cash value is considered 'on cash basis' and not taxable. Loans do not deplete your cash value, please recall. Your loan is made by the insurance company and collateralized by your cash value, which is why you never take out a policy loan greater than available cash value amounts.

The death benefit is tax-free and requires no probate to your beneficiaries.

And in your retirement years? You can withdraw regularly in an 'unrepaid policy loan' without having your withdrawn amount count against your Social Security income – so no tax burden is added here, either. You're withdrawing your own money. This is much, much more advantageous than withdrawals from your 401k at age 70!

Not Starting Wealthy? Good!

Remember that you don't need to be a wealthy person to own these policies. There is no minimum/maximum to pay into such policies; the only limitation is the amount of death benefit the insurer grants. In fact, you can tell your agent how much you'd like to pay in quarterly or annual premiums and let the agent do the math; they'll 'back into' the amount of death benefit you can get at that premium rate. (See Michael Anthony's Case Study in that chapter, where he did just that). You simply seek as high a cash value policy as you can afford.

If you are not the insured (not qualified medically), you can name another person as insured; you remain the policy owner and as such control the policy while insuring this other individual. The insured party is <u>not</u> the most important aspect of such policies; you establish the policy, so you own it. <u>Your ownership</u> of the policy is the most important thing.

CHAPTER 9

CHARTS & SCENARIOS

"You who are young, be happy while you are young,
and let your heart give you joy in the days of your youth.
Follow the ways of your heart and whatever your eyes see,
but know that for all these things God will bring you into judgment."
Ecclesiastes 11:9

I know people learn and understand concepts in different ways, and that 'a picture is worth a thousand words'. In this chapter I am providing visual aids – tables that show you how your money grows – as both Cash Value that you can take as loans during the policy's duration at any time, and as Death Benefit accruing for your chosen beneficiary. Look at this in the context of 'the numbers don't lie' – the numbers tell the truth about what is happening to your money!

Please look at the charts and explanations, as they take you through the numbers and prove out the superiority of this personal money-management and wealth-building solution.

Percentages vs Dollars

I'd like to make a few comments about percentages versus dollar amounts, and real profits versus paper profits.

In any stock market crash, people are thrilled to see that their stock or their whole account is 'up 12%'. They are contrarily in despair about the 'losses' their account takes when the market plummets by as much or more. To be happy about a profit is natural, just as frustration at a loss is human.

But ... Losses? Yes and no. They don't remember a key point about investing. They had 'paper' profits only, not real bankable ones! Until you take the money out of the profitable stock and deposit it in your account as cash, you do not *have* any profits! It's all a theoretical gain.

In the financial industry, we speak of a 'realized' gain – meaning that you saw your stock profiting and cashed out. The cash is in your hands; it is realized. However, if you have lost your principle in the markets, that's quite another thing. That is most definitely not a paper loss but a realized loss, and that means *there is no cash* to deposit at the bank!

Next, rates of return are typically expressed as percentages. It's a great way that we can use math to compare apples to apples. However, you cannot deposit a percentage in your bank account. You cannot pay your child's tuition with a percentage. You don't pay off that mortgage on your home with a percentage. You need *cash dollars*, and we all know it, in spite of our emphasis on the percentage values that our investments are up or down.

That is why I avoid the percentage game in these charts. Just look at the dollars you pay in (premiums and extra cash you can devote to this long-term endeavor). Look at the dollars accrued as net cash value of your policy. Look at the growing death benefit amount of dollars that can be paid out to a beneficiary. You don't deposit or spend a percentage – but you <u>can</u> deposit and spend, borrow and pay out dollars.

Keep this in mind as you decipher the charts. I will explain each one as I go along.

Funding a Policy

You won't need to know anything about insurance underwriting as a policy owner, but you should understand the 'moving parts' of this transaction, so that you are comfortable 'operating your bank' (which is your dividend-paying whole life insurance policy with riders).

The first moving part you'll be asked to look at is **funding the policy.** This can happen in basically three ways as I have stated, regardless of the size of the death benefit you can afford (or that the insurance company can grant you given their internal guidelines).

Let's start with the first, classic way: paying in a fixed premium amount every year for 30 years. (I will only show 29 years in my charts, as my fictitious policy owner has only decided to become his own banker at age 41 or so…).

Keep in mind that a high value policy (the $20,000 per year in premiums may not be reachable for all of us) such as I am illustrating may be too much for you at this time. Look at the charts anyway as a demonstration of how your money grows safely, predictably. Remember that the current cash value of your dividend-paying whole life insurance policy remains available to you whatever its amount, for policy loans. The charts will not show any policy loans until the retirement years, and those loans are not repaid but fund your retirement costs of living (first 2 scenarios). We assume for these illustrations a 5% internal growth.

Policy Year	Age/End of Yr	Annual Outlay START of Yr	Net Cash Value END of Yr	Net Death Benefit END of Yr
1	41	$20,000	$18,365	$951,544
2	42	$20,000	$38,520	$970,298
3	43	$20,000	$59,491	$1,003,148
4	44	$20,000	$80,899	$1,034,194
5	45	$20,000	$102,752	$1,063,707
6	46	$20,000	$123,990	$1,088,280
7	47	$20,000	$146,486	$1,114,154
8	48	$20,000	$170,333	$1,141,433
9	49	$20,000	$195,619	$1,169,739
10	50	$20,000	$222,409	$1,199,103
11	51	$20,000	$250,770	$1,229,586
12	52	$20,000	$280,730	$1,261,207
13	53	$20,000	$312,411	$1,294,234
14	54	$20,000	$345,877	$1,328,719
15	55	$20,000	$381,258	$1,364,941
16	56	$20,000	$419,434	$1,404,916
17	57	$20,000	$460,514	$1,448,531
18	58	$20,000	$504,725	$1,195,915
19	59	$20,000	$552,203	$1,546,595
20	60	$20,000	$603,109	$1,600,625
21	61	$20,000	$657,336	$1,656,604
22	62	$20,000	$714,570	$1,714,916
23	63	$20,000	$774,917	$1,775,824
24	64	$20,000	$838,493	$1,839,481
25	65	$20,000	$905,461	$1,905,902
26	66	$20,000	$975,910	$1,974,974
27	67	$20,000	$1,050,087	$2,046,781
28	68	$20,000	$1,128,142	$2,121,084
29	**69**	**$20,000**	**$1,210,266**	**$2,198,013**
30	70	$0	**$1,275,767**	$2,068,296
31	71	$0	**$1,344,626**	$2,129,291
32	72	$0	**$1,416,924**	$2,192,600
33	73	$0	**$1,492,833**	$2,259,028
34	74	$0	**$1,572,548**	$2,328,528
35	75	$0	**$1,656,142**	$0
36	76	($120,000)	$1,617,371	$2,296,945
37	77	($120,000)	$1,576,017	$2,193,757
38	78	($120,000)	$1,532,041	$2,091,467

CHART #1 = Steady as You Go Scenario

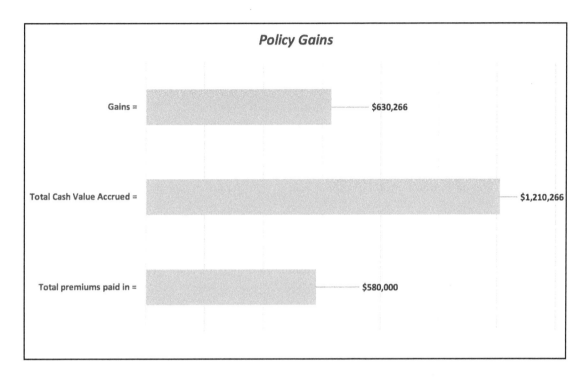

Policy Gains

Gains = — $630,266

Total Cash Value Accrued = — $1,210,266

Total premiums paid in = — $580,000

This first chart's progression assumes a regular, unchanging annual premium payment of $20,000.

Over 29 years, the total premiums you will have paid in equal $580,000. At the end of Year 29 – when you are 69 years old – the total Cash Value your policy will have accrued is $1,210,266. Again, not using any percentages, your cash gain is $630,266 ($1,210,266 - $580,000). You can rejoice at that **tax-free gain.**

The **red** numbers, starting at your age 76, in the 3rd column, are unrepaid policy loans that you decided you need to take to fund your retirement. In other words, at age 76 you start taking policy loans from the Cash Value to fund your retirement, with no intention of repaying the loans, and do so for the remaining 19 years you live.

64

Policy Year	Age/End of Yr	Annual Outlay START of Yr	Net Cash Value END of Yr	Net Death Benefit END of Yr
1	41	$75,000	$71,834	$1,892,256
2	42	$75,000	$148,889	$2,098,007
3	43	$20,000	$176,003	$2,126,567
4	44	$20,000	$203,600	$2,152,987
5	45	$20,000	$231,600	$2,177,595
6	46	$20,000	$258,671	$2,195,894
7	47	$20,000	$287,258	$2,216,106
8	48	$20,000	$318,271	$1,800,770
9	49	$20,000	$351,200	$1,827,249
10	50	$20,000	$386,137	$1,855,599
11	51	$20,000	$423,251	$1,886,104
12	52	$20,000	$462,565	$1,918,746
13	53	$20,000	$504,252	$1,953,887
14	54	$20,000	$548,398	$1,991,574
15	55	$20,000	$595,186	$2,032,186
16	56	$20,000	$645,457	$2,077,604
17	57	$20,000	$699,334	$2,127,636
18	58	$20,000	$757,100	$2,182,462
19	59	$20,000	$818,923	$2,241,396
20	60	$20,000	$884,999	$2,301,520
21	61	$20,000	$955,470	$2,370,604
22	62	$20,000	$1,029,915	$2,440,155
23	63	$20,000	$1,108,482	$2,513,542
24	64	$20,000	$1,191,305	$2,590,911
25	65	$20,000	$1,278,608	$2,672,259
26	66	$20,000	$1,370,494	$27,395
27	67	$20,000	$1,467,320	$2,846,449
28	68	$20,000	$1,569,269	$2,939,046
29	**69**	**$20,000**	**$1,676,592**	**$3,035,348**
30	70	$0	$1,767,335	$2,865,237
31	71	$0	$1,862,731	$2,949,739
32	72	$0	$1,962,891	$3,037,449
33	73	$0	$2,068,053	$3,129,478
34	74	$0	$2,178,488	$3,225,765
35	75	$0	$2,294,296	$3,326,127
36	76	($160,000)	$2,247,161	$3,191,356
37	77	($160,000)	$2,196,789	$3,057,848
38	78	($160,000)	$2,143,128	$2,925,691

Keep in mind that you can decide you need less money than this for your expenses and so you withdraw a lesser sum each year. After all, using these policies, you have probably already paid off your home mortgages, and all the other big costs of living you have. You can certainly also start taking money sooner (say, from age 62 or 69), up to only the amount remaining as Cash Value. You can 'zero out' a policy in this way. There is no prohibition to doing so, and indeed many owners of two or more policies choose to do just this as they need to.

In this scenario, the total income you take, starting at age 76 and continuing for the remaining 19 years you live, is $120,000 x 19 = $2,280,000. The policy's Death Benefit is reduced to $568,137 (augmented by remaining Cash Value of $279,204) at that time.

In this very typical scenario, you stop paying premiums at age 70. My goal is to show you how the Cash Value keeps earning.

That is the first way to launch and continuously fund your policy.

CHART #2 = Partial Frontloading Scenario

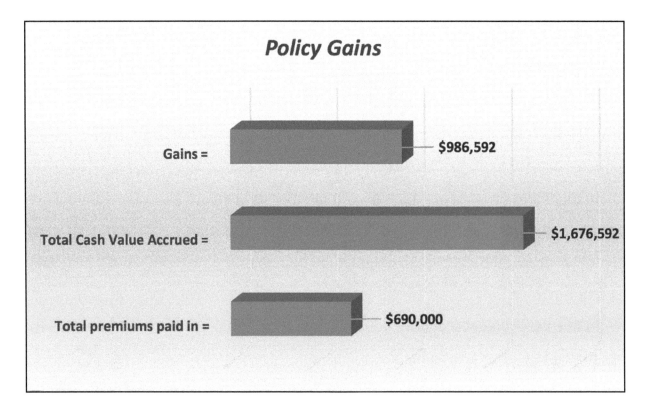

This chart shows us a second way to start out. It is for those of you with a lump sum of cash, say, from cashing out a non-performing 401k or IRA, and paying taxes due on it for that early withdrawal or account closure. The net sum that remains can be used to partially 'frontload' your policy.

In this partially frontloaded example, you have put together an extra lump sum (above and beyond the $20,000 premium amount you will also pay) of 2 times $55,000, which you add to the policy in years one and two. From then on, you carry on with only the contractual premium of $20,000.

But look now at the Year 29 line carefully. This is the year of your last premium payment; you are age 70. Over 29 years, the total premiums paid in equal $690,000. The total Cash Value accrued by Year 29 is $1,676,592. Your **tax-free**

gain is $986,592 ($1,676,592 - $690,000). The originally contracted Death Benefit of $1M has grown to $3,035,348 by the end of Year 29.

You have decided that you can wait in this scenario until age 76 to start taking income via unrepaid policy loans from the policy's Cash Value to fund your retirement for the remaining (hypothetically) 19 years of your life. Your total income taken (from age 76 to your death) is $160,000 x 19 years or $3,040,000!

As you reduce the Cash Value through unrepaid policy loans, the Death Benefit at your death is reduced accordingly – in this case to $994,065 (augmented by remaining Cash Value of $573,466). Still nearly a million dollars – tax-free, probate-free – for your heir(s)!

Again, in your later years, will you need or want $160,000 per year? You don't have a crystal ball to predict the cost of living, the state of your health, your wishes to spend money on experiences and legacies (world cruises, charitable foundations…) and so on. But this scenario demonstrates that you can take out and spend that much if you want or need to! And if you don't need to? The Death Benefit will be a larger amount for the beneficiaries you have named.

Policy Year	Age/End of Yr	Annual Outlay START of Yr	Net Cash Value END of Yr	Net Death Benefit END of Yr
1	41	$75,000	$72,052	$1,867,850
2	42	$75,000	$149,182	$2,085,198
3	43	$0	$155,462	$2,046,667
4	44	$0	$161,089	$2,006,787
5	45	$0	$165,993	$1,965,740
6	46	$0	$168,902	$1,919,539
7	47	$0	$171,816	$1,874,995
8	48	$0	$175,837	$1,235,411
9	49	$0	$180,151	$1,197,544
10	50	$0	$184,766	$1,161,400
11	51	$0	$195,274	$540,506
12	52	$0	$206,375	$553,137
13	53	$0	$218,101	$566,216
14	54	$0	$230,477	$579,773
15	55	$0	$243,550	$593,909
16	56	$0	$257,364	$608,727
17	57	$0	$271,955	$624,195
18	58	$0	$287,370	$640,378
19	59	$0	$303,653	$657,130
20	60	$0	$320,835	$674,477
21	61	$0	$338,953	$692,475
22	62	$0	$358,058	$711,264
23	63	$0	$378,182	$730,942
24	64	$0	$399,362	$751,556
25	65	$0	$421,665	$773,113
26	66	$0	$445,098	$795,572
27	67	$0	$469,751	$818,952
28	68	$0	$495,681	$843,181
29	**69**	**$0**	**$522,932**	**$868,283**
30	70	$0	$551,567	$894,211
31	71	$0	$581,652	$921,079
32	72	$0	$613,207	$948,899
33	73	$0	$646,309	$978,026
34	74	$0	$681,027	$1,008,420
35	75	$0	$717,397	$1,040,038
36	76	$0	$755,475	$1,072,904
37	77	$0	$795,119	$1,106,777

Early In, Earns More

Let's compare these first 2 scenarios now. Compare the line for Year 29 on these first two charts. See that in the partially frontloaded scenario of Chart #2, you have more money in the policy earlier – *$110,000 more*. That higher amount of '*early bird money*' grows through compounding for a longer period of time. Thanks to more years of compounding, you earn more. Thus, the 2nd scenario – partial front-loading – has earned you *$466,326 more* in Cash Value than the 1st scenario of even and regular premium payments.

This is why the best insurance agent will encourage you to
find the extra cash to partially or fully frontload
your dividend-paying whole life insurance policy.

CHART #3 = Fully Frontloading Scenario

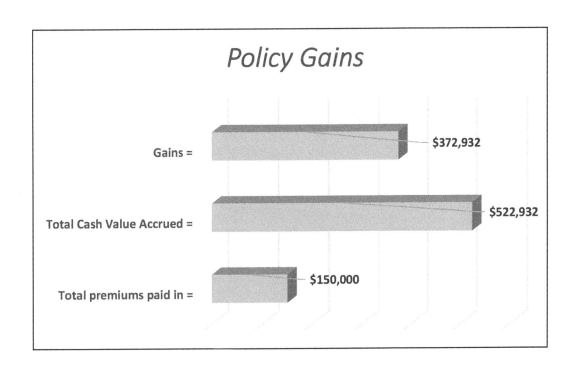

In this third scenario, I would like to show the 'fully frontloaded' policy. Over 29 years your total premiums paid in equals just $150,000. In fact, you only paid in $75,000 two times – in years one and two of the policy's existence. At the end of Year 29, when you are 69 years old, the total Cash Value accrued is $522,932, representing cash gains/profits to you of $372,932 in tax-free, fully accessible cash.

You have stopped paying premiums after 2 years, but the policy remains active, receives dividend payments and continues to grow in value.

You notice that you make no Policy Loans, as in the prior two scenarios. You have no crystal ball, but you when took out this policy you held the forward-looking assumption that "it is better to have and not need, than need and not have". This simply shows you that – should you need it – the cash is there for you.

This scenario of no loans (repaid or unrepaid) can also exist when you have a number of policies and, as it happens, you did not use this particular one for loans. What remains is a solid Life Insurance legacy amount for your chosen beneficiaries – you are leaving a Death Benefit of **$2,164,672** and as always with these policies, it is tax-free and probate-free to the beneficiaries.

CHAPTER 10

CASE STUDIES – REAL PEOPLE, REAL MONEY, REAL LIFE STORIES

"So then, banish anxiety from your heart and cast off the
troubles of your body, for youth and vigor are meaningless."

Ecclesiastes 11:10

You can in fact become your own banker.

If using this tool has, in our day and age, been a *Less-Than-1%-Club*, I want you to realize that it is not reserved for billionaires! It is not reserved for the wealthy at all – but you have seen than you can develop a degree of wealth and enjoy the lifestyle of the wealthy by using it as it was designed.

<u>Remember</u>: Our grandparents and forefathers were already using – before we were born – the dividend-paying cash value whole life policy with its riders just like we are learning to do. The advent of the 401k and the internet making self-directed stock investment so easy (but unfortunately for most of us, not that profitable) that it took our attention away from how ***to be sole proprietor of our own bank***! We can get back to that and teach our children how as well.

> *Become Your Own Banker.*
> *And Never Again "a Borrower or Lender*
> *Be" – Unless You Borrow from or Lend*
> *to* <u>*Yourself!*</u>

<u>Remember</u>: The life insurance industry is the one with the best track record and staying power of all our industries. By choosing to work with the best of that great industry, you are ensuring the success of your own private 'bank' for decades and even generations to come.

<u>Remember</u>: Managing your own money and turning it into wealth is not really The Secret of the Ages that it seems to have become. It's not rocket science, either. You don't need an advanced degree or even be that great at basic arithmetic to make this the primary way you manage your hard-earned money and let it work hard for you. Our grandparents were 'just folks' and they figured it out. So can we.

To further deepen your understanding of how powerful this tool is to having personal control over your money, your family's and your business's well-being, I am sharing examples of how I and a number of my clients are using this miracle tool. My hope is that these examples will inspire you to take charge of your money. You have been working so hard to make it, I know and appreciate this.

It is time to make your money work for you – like a banker does – and stop working so hard for your money!

Case Study: Dr. Chinyere Orafu

Chinyere Orafu is a board-certified Obstetrician-Gynecologist (Ob-Gyn) in private traditional practice and is a board-certified surgeon. She additionally owns and operates a cosmetic/laser practice providing non-invasive or minimally invasive care and operates that business in 2 locations.

Today, the doctor owns 5 policies. One insures her, and her company owns it; one is on herself that she owns; she also owns a total of three policies on her children (2 on her daughter; 1 on her son) for which she is the beneficiary. Here are her thoughts on such wealth-building and money-management tools:

"Skeptics might say that life insurance is a waste of their hard-earned money and only gets the insurance company rich. That is simply not true with these products. Was I initially skeptical? Yes and no. I initially thought it was one of those 'too good to be true' things when I first heard about it. But when a professional in the industry tells you it is rock solid, and shows you the numbers that prove it, you have to pay attention.

I am a businesswoman, so I got two opinions on this instrument. My first talk was with Lucien who was very positive about it. I got a second opinion and that person advised against it. So, I did some additional research on my own, too, and along with Lucien's further presentation, I was convinced of the possibilities. I contracted for my first policy and then the others. As I think back, if I'd listened to the negative reviewer of the product, I would have lost hundreds of thousands of dollars since that time!

I contracted policies for my business to internally (or self-) finance the rather expensive equipment it needs. Each piece of equipment we use runs from $75,000 to $145,000 in purchase value. Since owning these policies, I have taken out five large policy loans to buy equipment. I pay all the loans back with interest.

My feeling about this tool? I recommend it to all business owners who take the longevity and growth of their business operations seriously. I would also tell business owners to work with an experienced, informed agent; not every agent is going to give sound advice, simply because he or she has not benefitted from specific training in these investment instruments.

As for the personal policies, I have two children. I got the policies on them and I am policy owner. My strategy is that these policies will be used for their future car purchases and college tuition needs. You always hope your child will be awarded a scholarship, but even then, such awards don't cover everything! In this way, as a parent, I am hoping for the best and planning for the worst, as it were.

I contracted those three policies when the children were younger than 10; they are 15 and 14 now. The policies still have plenty of time to develop significant cash value for the purposes I intended.

Listen, this tool is not reserved for the very rich and I am proof. When I got my start, I was a debt-burdened new physician! I started out small with these investment tools. Don't let the amount of money you *don't have now* get in the way of building wealth for yourself. I shudder to think of how high my current business debt would be if I had listened to that nay-sayer about these policies.

In fact, the whole concept is not to *start* rich, but to *end up* wealthy, and to be your own funder, whatever it is you want to buy. Your money is protected from market fluctuations, so that you don't have the shock of having no money left when you need it most. The beauty of this instrument is that your small amounts are protected as they grow, and that there is no risk to your principle or gains – the money will always be there."

Case Study: Todd Colucy

Sometimes even industry professionals resist the idea that they can be their own bankers – their own wealth-builders and money-lenders – *this easily*. That was the case for this gentleman! Todd is a CPA and former Kent State University adjunct professor. Although we are in related professional fields, we didn't meet during any industry event, but at our church. Here in his own words is what he has done with this tool:

"I'm just naturally curious about 'how money works' and the best use of my money to make it work for me. There is a school of thought that says, "Buy term insurance and invest the difference elsewhere." But then, just as my parents were all set to retire, I saw them lose their retirement funds which were in the stock market. It was in 2008. The Big Crash. It was truly an eye-opener for me about the security (or lack thereof) of our money.

I was always told that Whole Life Insurance was a rip-off. Yet there are whole life products (now I know this) which are phenomenal for letting me be my own bank.

My own Financial Advisor tried for 12 years to talk me into purchasing one of these wealth-building whole life policies and I resisted … I told myself that because it was not mainstream it just had to be a shaky proposition. I said, "How can it be so great if so few people are using it?"

My First Policy

I was in my mid-40s and a father of two teens getting ready for college when I finally got my first dividend-paying cash value whole life policy, written up with the necessary riders and its 'operation' fully explained to me.

Very, very soon, I was wishing I had done this earlier! Ah, hindsight…

I am a trained CPA; at this writing, I've just recently left my position of Adjunct Professor at Kent State University, teaching Accounting and Introduction to Corporate Finance. Today I am involved in Dave Ramsey's Financial Peace program; our church offers the class once yearly and I facilitate it. Should I have known better, should I have known sooner about the wealth-building power of these whole life policies? Yes, but like lots of my fellow CPAs, we know finance well, but not so much about personal finance as concerns wealth-building.

So, I initially took out just one policy, specifically to fund my children's education. I took out all the equity on my house and front-loaded / funded the policy with that amount.

The student loan system allows the student to borrow up to $5,000, but then it is on us, the parents, to borrow the rest – at 7% interest. I'd had this first policy only 2 years at the time I took out that initial policy loan for my older child's tuition needs. I repeated this with my second child's education. And all the while, my cash value was not only 100% intact, but growing due to both the premiums I continued to pay in, the accrued cash value due to the loan interest I paid, and the dividend that was annually added to the cash value.

Since then, the kids have both bought cars with a policy loan from this same policy of mine; our deal was that they make the agreed monthly payments directly back into the policy for me. True, it doesn't help build their personal credit since they are basically 'invisible borrowers', but I made sure they are building their credit in other traditional ways that are visible.

Why I Own Multiple Policies

I now have three policies. The two additional policies are just to build wealth! I definitely know where my money is all the time – and how much I have – unlike my parents and so many others who are hoping that their money will be there, in the amounts they planned on, when they are ready to retire.

The second two policies are instead of banking the cash I have, and instead of socking it somewhere in the stock markets. It's the best wealth-building tool out there.

Do I advise to always invest in your employer 401k to the maximum (assuming you have that option)? Yes, definitely! And then – do this with the rest of your cash!

Right now, I'm getting a 5.4% annual dividend payment on my policies and have an interest rate of 4.5% on any and all policy loans I take out. Those rates don't budge. The spread earns me money – just like a bank earns via the spread. I've got some money invested in a great project I was introduced to and I'm getting a 12% return on the money I've invested in it. To have funds to invest, I took a policy loan from my second policy at the 4.5% interest rate. You may think that 12% minus 4.5% gives me my gain, but it is not in fact a 7.5% return that I am getting! It is actually a 166% return. (12% - 4.5% is 7.5. 7.5 net/4.5 cost is 166% return.) Plus, I'm still getting my dividends on that policy's 100% intact cash value.

As for the third policy, I had an old 401k. I took advantage of the IRS 72T program. I paid the income tax on the amount I withdrew from the 401k but had no penalty to pay under the 72T. I'm not paying that amount back into my 401k (which would be typical), but I will still not be penalized. I used it to pay policy premiums on that third policy."

Case Study: Michael Anthony

Michael Anthony is superintendent with the Eastern Caribbean district of ministry. I met him when I was invited to share what I know from the world of personal finance and investing with his congregation – tips that could empower people in their lives as well as do more of the Kingdom Work of God. Here in his own words is how Michael himself is now using the dividend-paying cash value whole life insurance policy with riders as his own personal and private bank:

"Lucien explained to our gathering how we could have our own loan financing – be our own banker – with this tool. I was interested right away – because what non-profit or congregation could not use more cash for its good works?

However, my first roadblock (or so I thought) was that I failed the medicals to cover my own life! I'd had an older history of asthma and mini strokes some years before, now healed. I'm 60 today and fit as a fiddle; I swim a quarter mile with ease, but there you go. I fell into that 'uninsurable' category with the insurance underwriters.

But I remembered what Lucien said, and I contracted a policy on my 29-year-old niece with whom I have a friendly relationship. She was the insured and I was the policy owner. She passed the medicals as we both knew she would, and I was off and ready to be my own banker. My niece did this as a favor to me knowing I would be the sole borrower.

I was now 'sole proprietor' of my own bank. Heady stuff!

You Don't Have to Have Millions to Do This

You might think that I have tons of money at my disposal to do something like this, but Lucien explained to us that day in church that anyone can do it, at any income level. There are life insurance policies for a wide range of death benefit dollar amounts, and a correspondingly wide range of premium amounts.

I contracted the policy with Security Mutual of New York, with myself as policy owner. I took out the policy about 3 years ago (2015-16?). I make $3,000 in quarterly premium payments. You see that the annual premium comes to $12,000; I contracted, however, to pay quarterly. Like a car insurance or home insurance policy, you can pay monthly, quarterly or annually. No need for me to wait for a year to build cash value in my policy!

My budget (that premium amount) allowed for a policy death benefit of $850,000. My $3,000 quarterly premiums allow a <u>maximum</u> pay-in of $3,600/quarter. I pay in the maximum when I can, since there is no obligation to do so. I apply some of the premium to the riders.

From this single policy, I have lent myself as much as $18,000. I use the money for business things and pay it back quarterly or at least according to the pre-agreed schedule. I never default. I'm never late. I've never paid a penalty. I know the rules. I can pay back or not pay the loan. But I always choose to pay back with interest.

Just over a month ago, I took out my most recent policy loan. At the time of the prior premium payment, my cash value was at just $800. To be able to make myself this loan, I made my maximum pay-in at premium time of $3,600, which served to bump the cash value up to $4,400. That is how I easily took out a policy loan of $3,100, or, as I like to say because it makes me smile, "I made myself a loan of $3,100!".

I find this very simple and straightforward: Keep your premiums up and it goes very easily. Pay back the loans on time and it goes very easily. I know my policy status in real time; my statements are viewable online anytime and show my real-time numbers. If next week I pay the $3,100 back? I can borrow again, up to whatever cash value I have on the books!

As Lucien revealed this tool to us, he told us that this is where the big Wall Street brokers get all their money to risk on the Stock Exchange! They each have many multi-million-dollar policies to pull that off, but Lucien revealed one other attractive side to this personal banking options: It is <u>not</u> a tool just for the vastly wealthy. I've already proved that to myself.

I'm now getting ready to take out a second policy. I want this one for an 11-year old boy as the covered party, and this time I will make the child's mother the policy owner. I will pay the agreed premiums for it and give her the 'sole banking proprietorship' and decision-making control. This is an extremely flexible tool that can allow us to benefit others in such a way!

Lucien and I discussed the options for this policy: He asked about the premium I wanted to pay ($1,000/quarter). He crunched the numbers and told me that $1,250/quarter was more optimum, so I'll do that instead. We'll decide on a death benefit amount when we look at a firm contract. My son – being just 11 now and with 6-7 years to run before heading off to college – will be able to take out policy loans (or rather, his mom will, as she will be the owner of the policy) for his college tuition and other expenses! The policy will be sizeable enough at that time for his needs. He can work for pocket money if he chooses, but he'll be assured that the 'big bills' are covered. His mom can rest easy on this, too.

Once I have that set up for them, I'm taking the concept to more congregation members. I'll have personal experience of this Sole Proprietor Banker to share with them as proof that this is not just a tool for someone with deep pockets. As you can imagine, this group of people is in a wide age and health spectrum. It doesn't matter if they cannot insure themselves; I'll tell them what I did. I'll explain the ease of borrowing. Then, they can decide how best to become a Sole Proprietor Banker, too. I view this as one outstanding way for me and Lucien to minister to the whole man.

Case Study: Me, Lucien Stephenson

You would not be happy with me if I told you about this wealth-building and money-management tool without revealing that I, too, hold such policies! And naturally, I do. But not for as long a time as I would have liked, actually...

I personally now own three policies: Two cover my life and one that covers my son.

The first policy is one I converted from term life insurance to whole life. The term life premium was $246/quarter ($1,139 annually). After the conversion, the annual premium was $17,000. Yes, it was a big jump, but by the time I converted the policy, my income had also jumped, and I could afford it.

Why did I have term insurance at all? Initially, I really needed life insurance (I was a father of two children by then). I simply could not afford the $1M death benefit I thought I needed for the family in a whole life policy. I could not pull it off at that time in my career and at that level of earnings. So, I bought the term policy since I could afford $246 four times a year.

Term life insurance is also known as 'pure insurance': You give the life insurance company one dollar and they give you $1,000 of death benefit. You choose the policy duration or 'term'; the policies can run for 10, 20 or 30 years. Once the term of your policy expires, you typically have several choices: renew for another term, convert to permanent coverage (called whole life insurance – this is what I did), or allow the policy to expire. The term policy is typically convertible to a whole life policy within 10 years, therefore allowing the insured to fulfill the need for actual whole life insurance in the future when they can afford to make the premium payments.

If you think about when most people contract for a term policy, it is when they become a parent. They want (just like I did) to make sure the family is taken care of if they die when the children are still minors. They calculate for the policy to expire when the children reach age 21 or so. Thus, 90% of total term policies never pay the death benefit – and you can imagine how the insurance carriers love that! Since most Americans don't die until after age 60, you see that it is long after most term insurance they might have contracted has ended, so there is no death benefit payout.

Uninsurable? Not an Issue!

Since I have multiple sclerosis, I could not get life insurance coverage on my own person today; I would definitely not pass the medical exam!

When I purchased that term insurance (with a death benefit of $1 million), I got a contract that was convertible to whole life. That is the way I could not only afford the coverage, but how I could get any whole life insurance on myself today at all.

Most or all of the life insurance I sell is convertible to whole life with a term insurance rider as described in these pages; you might just check any term life insurance policies you hold to see if they, too, are convertible. That could be (like it was for me) a great way to get started with the Sole Proprietor Banking yourself.

The other policy – the one on my son – is more recent; that has a quarterly premium of $3,000. He is healthy; I am the beneficiary/owner of the policy, so my own health is not an issue.

CONCLUSION

"Of making many books there is no end, and much study wearies the body.

Now all has been heard; here is the conclusion of the matter:

Fear God and keep his commandments, for this is the duty of all mankind.

For God will bring every deed into judgment, including every

hidden thing, whether it is good or evil."

Ecclesiastes 12:12-14

Yes, even the industry professionals and savvy businesspeople may look with skepticism (but also with wonder) at the wealth-building, money-management tool I have been describing. But they do come around, as the stories Todd Colucy and Chinyere Orafu told shows!

You have seen how easy it is to be admitted as a member of the *Less-Than-1%-Club* - even with as little upfront investment as Michael Anthony made.

If this 1% Club way to increase your wealth is not amazing enough, all your dollars are now tax-free – forevermore. Whether you access your own money through Policy Loans that you pay back or that you do not, at no time is that money taxable! You cannot do that with other IRS-approved tax-deferred vehicles such as a 401k.

The Case Studies have hopefully also demonstrated that you do not need lots of cash to get started. Remember that you do *not* need to be wealthy to use this instrument. Not at all! After all, the goal is to become *wealthy* by becoming the *Sole Proprietor of your own Bank* – and to have more and more *tax-free dollars* available to you all throughout your life right into your retirement years.

The more tax advantages, the better, right? Thus, if you are involving your business, I would also recommend that you consult with your business CPA (or find a good one through referrals) to determine the potential tax-deductibility of the insurance premiums you'll pay on a business-benefitting policy.

I believe you should buy as much Dividend-Paying Cash Value Whole Life Insurance with Riders from a mutual insurance company as the company will allow – and as much as you can afford at the time. Start by calculating the ceiling of how much you can afford to pay in annual premiums, based on your income now. Ask yourself if you'd be better off paying quarterly premiums or annual ones. Remember that you can always contract for an additional policy when you are earning more or have any sort of windfall monies drop in your lap!

Take a serious look at any lump-sum savings you now have (CDs or savings accounts at the bank; 401k accounts, accrued savings from passive real estate holdings, etc.). What interest or return are you earning on it? Probably nothing like this investment vehicle can provide! If you have lump sums to apply to a new policy, think about contracting a policy that you frontload. It is a seriously profitable way to build your wealth!

YOUR NOTES

YOUR NOTES

YOUR NOTES

CPSIA information can be obtained
at www.ICGtesting.com
Printed in the USA
BVHW020624240620
582210BV00011B/198

9 781545 678732